SHAH RUKH KHAN
And Winds of Fire - A Memoir
By Sayan Roy

SHAH RUKH KHAN AND WINDS OF FIRE - A MEMOIR

First edition. September 15, 2021.

Copyright © 2021 Sayan Roy.

ISBN: 979-8224723911

Written by Sayan Roy.

Table of Contents

'To God and to everyone'

Preface

Certain things, and most importantly good things, should be talked about and discussed more often because it is necessary. Talking is important because there are lessons to be learned from good deeds that transcend our morality and actions as human beings. Psychology is a powerful tool, and when the work and actions of many people come together, change is inevitable. But it often takes a leader, an inspiration, a singular idea, or a collective concept to flick up that one desire to change, which will start the transformation process. This work of critical analysis is about how the legendary actor-humanitarian Shah Rukh Khan brought about a national transformation and became a global phenomenon in no time, which many believe came from a combination of hard work and luck. This work has been created after extensive research and scientific observation of the effects that the man had over the decades.

Shah Rukh Khan is where our lives, our imaginations and our hopes found deep colors – we whistled at theatres, we smiled at homes looking at the actor who always made us smile! This book is an acknowledgment, a tribute, a painful penning of nostalgia that made our school, college and life days shiningly brighter – a tribute to one and only Shahrukh Khan! He made us laugh, he made us sing, he is the one who made us run to theatres with fever and cry – bringing smile to our lips, dreams to our eyes; and so many years went by watching his films that made us fly! If love is a feeling that count stars and promises infinite, Shahrukh Khan is the feeling without which love is and will be incomplete! Here with my own shaky hands, I write with such trembling memories of lost childhood and struggling to make one the happiness and sadness of SRK memories – things that bought families and people closer and made us grow and live through changing times of neo-liberal India!!

'The philosopher creates, he doesn't reflect.' – Gilles Deleuze

'Life is irreversible and so is Shah Rukh Khan's love affair with India'

Chapter 1

The Beginning

SHAH RUKH KHAN ENTERED the industry in the early 1990s, and his transition from television to the big screen of Indian film was one of the most significant events of those years. It remains the most outstanding transition ever made. Shah Rukh Khan was famous among Indian audiences right from his television days when he played Fauji in the serial Fauji, aired on the national channel Doordarshan (DD National). It is the exceptional human persona that often has a strong presence and a majestic form of charm which carries humanity with it, and it was Shah Rukh Khan's beginnings with human race that was to change India forever. The charismatic appearance, strong screen presence, and ability to pull out iconic villainous performances were like a missing link to many viewers. This forced people to think of the actor differently, and hence, the line of difference was created. The actor showed his unique ability to leave the audience dazed, and he could make everybody fall in a strange likeness with him that went far beyond the audience's likeness or dislikeness for the film. In a way, people went to see 'Shah Rukh Khan' on the screen regardless of their genre preferences and in the process, developed a strong regard for Shahrukh's unique action skills. This kind of positive audience perception started to be seen as a rare incident for somebody who has just arrived at the silver screen. This rare but strong connection between Shah Rukh and the common people was only the inception of something highly unfathomable. Initially, it was the good social perception around the actor that laid foundation for the building of much bigger Shah Rukh Khan phenomenon in the upcoming years. Again, the growing love of audiences for Shahrukh was the key.

The remarkable talent of this man to mesmerize everybody and the return appreciation from audiences that often goes beyond adjectives made his unimaginable journey possible. It is understandable for the senior actors who already had some recognition among the Indian audience to enjoy this kind of remarkable connection but destiny chose Shah Rukh Khan, and thus came the 'Age of Shah Rukh Khan'. A lot of accidental factors played a great role in creation of the 'SRK phenomenon' and his choice of films came as unfathomable for many and thrillingly surprising for others. Firstly, the actor did films like Baazigar and Darr; he took up roles rejected by other actors and made them into such big hits that the world could not forget Shah Rukh Khan. And this also signifies the fact that the people from the film industry (actors, directors) who are considered to be more authentic film experts than general audience, these people who thought 'villainous hero' roles would not work out (at least in the Indian context) were wrong, dead wrong! The actor took up the difficult challenge of playing these unconventional roles and in turn, delivered some magnetic performances that are still celebrated even after thirty years! Yes, *Rahul Mehra* and *Ajay Sharma* – the two iconic villains of India cinema, Ajay Sharma being more of the anti-hero! The huge success of Darr and Baazigar also meant that critics started to become more engrossed with Shahrukh's fascinating works which amplified his stardom further.

Those early-day Shah Rukh Khan performances are so memorable that one can analyze them both deontologically and teleologically with equal interest and still have the same feelings of amazement! The cause that made him do the films and the outcomes of his actions that came from doing those films - made him the phenomenon that became an immortal rage amongst Indians and fans all over the world!! The actor's performances as *Rahul* in Darr and *Ajay* in Baazigar made him an overnight sensation—a career record that is envied by many even after all these years. In a matter of a decade, the whole country with all its states and people together, fell in love with the actor Shah Rukh Khan without knowing why they liked the person so much or whether he was to become the identity of the nation?! The concept of an antihero (as played in Baazigar) accidentally appealed to the country so much that he became 'The Shah Rukh Khan', India's new superstar. The actor became a superstar within four years of entering the Indian film industry, and this shows how fast a fire can run through the woods if the conditions are right. But the conditions were never truly set for him; he forced his way forward with a profound commitment towards acting, storytelling, and the wholesome radiation of enduring energy that set him apart! When it's written in the stars, you just have to clasp your hands and take a bow! and that's what created the era and aura of Shah Rukh Khan that lights up the skies even today!! People talk about critically acclaimed performances and serious film roles, but what about the unparalleled performances of Shah Rukh as a villain and anti-hero that could not be matched even after these long thirty years? Superstars who can act and actors who have become superstars are always rare in Indian cinema but Shahrukh is one such actor who could fuse art with commerce quite beautifully which made him into a world-encompassing spirit. The spirit of India moved with the spirit of SRK and this is one of the major reasons why the actor is not just a name but a phenomenon: Shah Rukh Khan became a rage, a mass celebration, and a gold superstar very early in his career, which was to change the face of the country.

Chapter 2

DDLJ and the establishment of stardom

There are some actors who just want to become stars; awards are not necessary for them, and then there are others who want to be recognized as actors rather than stars, then for them, artistic recognition is more important. Let us say there is another group of actors who too want awards to be recognized because they already think of themselves as great actors (in their own heads), but do not receive it! Then how do you describe the persona and the success of somebody who got both the blessings of bumper box office and good recognition for his artistic performances on the silver screen? Then ask yourself: What made this man exceptionally different from everybody else in the history of Indian cinema? It may be a peculiar connection with the audience, the choice of films, or rather the fact that he is the force of nature, as the French call it - *tour de force*! A fire that catches on and on, and one cannot do anything about it. Yes, for the year 1995, DDLJ (Dilwale Dulhania le Jayenge) won ten Filmfare awards and one national award. This was Shah Rukh's third Filmfare win in the best actor category (after *Baazigar* and *Kabhi Ha Kabhi Na*) and SRK's historic crossover from the legendary anti-hero to an undying lover-boy icon. The movie DDLJ not only changed the dynamics of Indian cinema but also gave India huge recognition on the platform of global cinema! DDLJ went against the old film-making technique of portraying the country and its film heroes in the darkness of turbid poverty or in the light of over-glorified family bonds. DDLJ made new things with conviction!!

Globalization in the neo-liberal era had already entered India then, and DDLJ in its true sense, became the first Indian movie to receive such a massive global reception, with Shah Rukh Khan becoming the 'Symbol of Love'. *Dilwale Dulhaniya Le Jayenge* was one of the very few Indian films to be mentioned in the prestigious '1001 Movies You Must See Before You Die' list. Such was its path-breaking global success, that it still runs at the Maratha Mandir even today! Some critics might say Filmfare was overtly partial to Shah Rukh and his film, but why should they be? The actor did not belong to any purple-blooded film family, nor did he have the money to buy the Filmfare platform, which has been highly revered since the 1950s. Still, leaving this unjust and irrational thought aside, how do they comprehend the immense global success of DDLJ? and its acceptance by a much larger global audience for such a long period of time to become the longest-running Indian film in history? The film gave hope and strength to many middle-class boys and girls to fight for their own lives and for the ones they are meant to be with, DDLJ defined the way of love in times when love marriages were a bigger stigma in Indian society that what it is now. Post-DDLJ success, the approach to filmmaking changed a lot in India, and movies became more focused on youth and families, which now held the ideas of globalization and more realistic social themes, particularly women's empowerment and diversity inclusion.

DDLJ is that one iconic film that every youth from every generation will always root for—for the revolution, the longing, the promises, and the cross-border love story of two iconic characters filmed in dreamy landscapes of Switzerland and green lushes of Punjab – which made love come true!! But apart from that, the social message of being supportive of the children in the family, supporting their choices, and understanding their feelings is all so strongly portrayed throughout the film – that it makes DDLJ feel special! Love marriage was a taboo in

Indian society then, and many men and women suffered from this problem in the country of that time which required a film of this caliber to empower individual choices and independence. While the concept of the film was not new, and while such ideas have already been idealized and realized many times in literature and older movies - it takes truly great actors and directors to make it feel in your veins! Some stories wait for protagonists to come alive, like DDLJ waited for Shah Rukh Khan to change the actor's destiny forever and India's conception of love forever!

Many people think of DDLJ as a romantic prodigy, but it has indeed more to offer. It is about seeing a dream and then fulfilling it, and we humans often do long for human touch, and dreams are not always material! This larger-than-life movie, in a true, honest way, showed us one of the basic meanings of life, which is to stand for our wishes and desires, and that two people who want to be with each other will always find a way, despite the world is with them or not!! And what to say about Shah Rukh Khan, the actor? The same actor who can torment you as a villain and consume you like a lover must be somebody extremely talented !! a man of a different league who was about to take on mankind and transcend them - The films which he made were merely his medium and his weapon!! That is why, to this day, he is not just a film star like others, but he is 'Shah Rukh Khan' 'the legend and the story' 'the emperor who conquered and became the eternal king of our hearts !!'

When you think of SRK, you see an immense wave of love and unthinkable popularity—a gold-ark filmography! DDLJ, DTPH, Kuch Kuch Hota Hai, Dil se, Om Shanti Om, Don you name it! It is there!! MNIK, Swades, Rab ne Bana di Jodi, Veer-Zaara – a wall full of silver accolades and bustling crackers all over! But there is a lot more involved in the process: backbreaking hard work, insane hours of overtime on the film sets, a deep passion for making people happy despite facing failures! Take or die – Shahrukh always had the ability to charm you again and again with different genres, and surviving the urge of pulling down anyone despite having the power to do so – made him the King in true words. Yes, Shah Rukh Khan has always been highly regarding of the film fraternity, the force that comes in togetherness, and having worked with different generations of actors, whether it is Farida Jalal Ji, Amrish Puri Ji or Zayed Khan, Amrit Arora, Shreyas Talpade - he always showered love, respect, and compassion on others. The power of a good actor comes from two fundamental things: passion and compassion! And these abilities never withered away from Shah Rukh Khan!!

He receives great love, vast power, and a unfailing belief from not only billions of fans but also from fellow actors, veteran actors, juniors, industrialists, media, and sportspersons which proves the fact that his movies made a difference at the highest level—his charming and enduring piece of art have somehow established a connection with what is known as 'collective unconsciousness' – the black void where we all are one. SRK has this phenomenon, which, at its core, is the collective form of empathy, love, and victory projected by millions of middle-class people who have seen their success in the success of SRK! There is a lot of vicarious learning and experiences of other people associated with SRK which made 'The Shah Rukh Khan phenomenon' possible, this journey of his could not have been possible without love – if he is one hand of his gold stardom, people are the other hand which only by joining completes the full circle! There might be a divine connection possible that keeps eternal the legend of SRK!! Actors who are much more talented could not such a connection but the fact is he did; he conquered what others could not, and that will always be the testimony, the supremacy, and lifeblood of the story that is 'Shah Rukh Khan'. You cannot deny the fact that SRK films, whether its DDLJ, Kuch Kuch Hota Hai, Chak de India, or Chennai Express, they have always united India from time to time, and that is why he has always been in many ways a Pan India Superstar.

Chapter 3

Late 90s and becoming of an icon

Shah Rukh Khan delivered hit after hit to cement his position as India's biggest star. In Kuch Kuch Hota Hai, Shah Rukh Khan left magic in Indian hearts and souls worldwide, which was to last forever. With the performance of a lifetime in Dil Se, Shah Rukh delivered one of his finest renderings as an artist, which gave rise to a cult fan-following of the movie itself. Mani Ratnam's masterpiece Dil Se (1998) and Johar's debut film Kuch Kuch Hota Hai (1998) were the first two Indian movies to make it to the United Kingdom BO Top 10, and at the crux of these legendary classics was the craft and repertoire of a man who could alter space-time continuity of films – taking art to rage and thoughts to fantasy!

Late 90s, this was probably the first time the name of Bollywood became synonymous with the name of Shah Rukh Khan. It takes some artistry to justify roles, but it takes great artistry to immortalise movie characters, so much so that audiences cannot separate the character from the actor! If seen deeply, the phantasmagorical aura of Shah Rukh Khan has been created by mainly five films, (which will be discussed later). The actor played these evergreen characters so well that it left the audiences bedazzled, and every person at some point resonated with the Shah Rukh films - dancing to the rhythm; musing with the songs! Shah Rukh Khan became the soul of India and its future global ambassador in the making. He toured around the world, marketing his films and himself too. The tickets sold like hotcakes showing the aura and magnanimity of the man who was taking Indian cinema to new heights across the borders.

Indian films and Indian culture were becoming globally known, and India was getting more prominent on the world map. Even if he was marketing himself, it is still difficult to establish that outré enduring connection with audiences who do not even understand your language— if not, it is out of love!! People love SRK, and somewhere there is a force involved that cannot be explained in earthly or in human terms – a force that comes from the skies and showers on some souls!!

With the multinational companies entering India in the 1990s, there was a rapid exchange of global communications, and the sales of many companies showed a significant rise with the brand image of SRK. Shah Rukh Khan was all over television with Cinthol, Mayur, and Hyundai Santro ads, and given his unearthly charm, his ads were endeared as much as his films. From advertisements to films to shows and television interviews, the actor reigned everywhere. With Chaiya Chaiya on everybody's lips and the 'Kuch Kuch Hota Hai dream' in everybody's eyes, Shah Rukh Khan became a household name - someone with whom everybody could relate. The aura of SRK marked the 90s era of India, and there was no turning back from there!

Chapter 4

New millennium and the metamorphosis

SRK characters are irreplaceable, and the superactor made them so real that people across diverse cultures and races still reverberate with the vibrations of those characters!! Raj Aryan Malhotra from the movie 'Mohabbatein' (2000), Sunil from *Kabhi Ha Kabhi Na* (1994), Devdas Mukherjee from *DevDas* (2002), Aman Mathur from *Kal Ho Na Ho* (2003), and Veer Pratap Singh from *Veer-Zaara* (2004) are some of the great instances when the actor got under the skin of these characters, making them more epic and more unforgettable for the audience! Whether it was ads, or a tele-film; or the old serials or the movies, Shah Rukh lives his part with utmost sincerity and loyalty - something only someone who is very calm, dedicated, and secure in its being and craft - can do.

The actor delivered hits, superhits, and blockbusters year after year, decade after decade, bringing a radical change in the culture and thought process of India. Coming back to his forte 'Romance' - the violin, and the faint smile on SRK's face in Mohabbatein were enough to make you believe in the powerful force of love—love alone, bordering on agape, spiritual, and deathless!!

The mist and fog around 'Gurukul' were the main components of the movie's cinematography, the same mist and fog also depicted the mystery of Raj Aryan. Shah Rukh Khan, as Raj Aryan, became the epitome of 'love and sacrifice' every time he appeared on the screen, he kept the hope alive for *Sameer*, *Vicky*, and *Karan* in pursuit of love, and this awakened the 'SRK' in each of us as the movie went by. They say that Shah Rukh can get into you very quickly, and the portrayal of Raj Aryan as a hopeful romantic, a promising youth who left everything for the girl he was in love with despite the fact she is no more - gave everybody goosebumps!! even the cold-blooded critics and cynics bled in the winds of SRK's romance! Only Shah Rukh can do that; only an actor of his dimension and class can transcend an entire generation and timeline with his unmatchable skills and enthusiasm for acting - Like Ajay in Baazigar, like Sunil in Kabhi Ha Kabhi Na, like Shah Rukh Khan lived the character of Raj Aryan Malhotra in Mohabbatein – it transcended our childhood and Indian cinema! And like history lives, aches and survives through the ages of living and dead, these deathless characters of Indian cinema will remain forever indelible as well!

The movie Mohabbatein was appreciated by critics and audiences alike, and it became a rage in those days. People across the country and students across the schools wore their sweaters around their shoulders and recited the dialogues most fondly —so much was the effect of this one in a lifetime, magical movie — it was really a one-of-a-kind film ever made in the Indian film industry. The enchantment weaved by Mohabbatein about 21 years back remains the same even in today's daylight! And, in the songs, in the scenes, and in its each minute segment, the movie carried the soul of Raj Aryan even if he is not there in the scenes – you know Raj Aryan somewhere looking for Megha!

One can say books should not be made into films, but many people would know about the book only by watching its film adaptation. Despite the plot being changed a bit and the storyline made more dramatized in the film adaptation (like many movies in this novel-to-film genre are mostly done) SRK's portrayal of Devdas remains one of the finest and most heart wrenching performances of the Indian film industry. If tragedy is the essence of Devadas's character, then Shah Rukh Khan humanized the book character through his masterclass repertoire of adroitness. Shah Rukh Khan lived *Devdas Mukerjee* like he did *Aman*.

A year later, a Shah Rukh Khan movie was about to break the hearts of the world; it was Shah Rukh Khan's role as Aman in the 2003 flick *Kal Ho Na Ho*. Watching the movie, it is so hard to say whether Shah Rukh is playing Aman or Aman is playing Shah Rukh. With eyes so sad and presence so charismatic, SRK delivers the best of his career - his life-like living of Aman on the silver screen that left a myriad of happy memories and traumatic scars on a billion hearts!! The character Aman was so clutching that he could harmonize everything around him with the feelings that he was feeling! Aman was empathic, courageous, and practical even during the most fearful and desolate times of life, and it was Shah Rukh Khan's life-affirming side that was captured in this ever-memorable role of happy-spirited Aman! Although romance and acting resides in blood and bones of the actor, still Aman was different! This movie comes as a superhuman effort on the part of Shah Rukh Khan to become Aman, but Aman is Shah Rukh, and therein lies the wonderful paradox of *Kal Ho Na Ho*!

The story of Kal Ho Na Ho depicts the story of a happy-go-lucky man entering the woods of death knowingly, with no choice left but to burn out! Aman keeps on helping others, even with the flames of his own life burning out with each ticking of the night's clock! Living to die, he takes on every moment of life optimistically and vows to live life happily spreading colors and courage to the broken families around him! He chose to help the lover of the girl he himself loved to get her and even in heart attacks and dark of the night ebbing towards him - he chose to make people smile who were complete strangers to him!! His love-hate relationship with Naina, his brotherhood with Rohit, and his being faithful son to Jennifer made us realize that love can go beyond blood and ties to bring transcendence and spiritual happiness everywhere!! Aman made Naina smile and made the love story possible for Rohit, and it was done so honestly and realistically that you forget it's a movie... It hits you like reality every time you watch KHKH, and this is where lies the prowess of Shah Rukh Khan, the great actor indeed!

Aman infuses the feeling of an undying charm of the man who cannot die, although he will have to, physically given his grave heart condition but not a single moment in the movie passes without the audience longing for more of Aman! With the human condition worsening and pain increasing, Shah Rukh Khan as cheerfully-dying Aman in the second half of Kal Ho Na Ho gave perhaps - the most powerful performance of Indian cinematic history!..- something that can change irrational haters and critics into die-hard fans! Aman not only comes out as an angel for Jiya, Rohit, and Naina but also for the broken part in each one of us! Aman was the victory of life in the face of death, a *pièce de résistance* that will be looked up to and learned from for many decades to come. Interestingly, the movie was not made to preach about disease or acting but to convey the simplest message: to live when you are alive, adding life to the years (like Aman sang 'Har pal iha ji bhar jio, jo hai sama aaa... kal ho na ho'). The actor in SRK was able to make the character Aman - an overpowering depiction of existentialism and a captivating act of endurance in the battle of life!

With successful films like *Kabhi Khushi Kabhi Gham, Chalte Chalte, Main Hoon Na,* and *Veer-Zaara,* Shah Rukh showed the versatility of his acting and stole the Indian hearts many times more - becoming what you know of him today - the King of Bollywood! The raging box office success and critical acclamation of his films made him someone who could dominate both sides of the film-world, commercial and artistic. This was intrinsically rare because most of the mainstream actors in India were not artistically successful, and many of the realistic film actors were not commercially successful. Hence, most of the time, when Indian audiences were divided into segments based on choices, they came together for a Shah Rukh Khan film. This is one of the major reasons behind his colossal success because, over the years, people of all ages and people from all walks of life did connect to Shah Rukh, and he could sell them 'essential, life-enhancing' lessons like love, friendship, hope, joy, and self-belief that happened to be an exclusive exchange during a cinematic watch. This quintessential exchange between Shah Rukh Khan and the audiences influenced many sociocultural and psychosocial changes in India – which made India known to be as 'Shahrukh Khan's country'! A matter of pride for all Indians who have grown up watching his works!

Popularity and compassion have been two long-time friends of SRK. This is something that you don't often see with actors — that they become household names and great life inspirations in a common man's life. Even in a film-crazy country like India, it is still rare that out of so many actors and other influential people who have come from different places, suddenly one would have such a strong impact on the lives of almost all common people that would go beyond films and turn into a maddening stardom like no other! But Shah Rukh was the first superstar to reach there! He broke the stereotype of a snobbish star who does not come out in public because he or she has a particular ego—a certain difference that keeps him higher than a common man. Breaking such prevalent stereotypes that came as a norm to the Indian film industry - is what made him the people's star in a realistic sense!! SRK came from the common mass and walked into common people to give them autographs and shake hands, and this is where people related to him as if he was their own! He became the upward projection of middle-class pride and truly the people's star!! He walked into the public freely, treating his fans like brothers and friends, and made films and art that was meant for all - hence having a powerful impact on the lives of people and on how they perceived life!

According to Gestalt psychology, human beings often perceive things in form of a pattern that eventually makes up something bigger for it have a bigger meaning. The concept of holism sits at the center of Gestalt psychology. If this is to be applied to the public perception of Shah Rukh Khan, it makes a greater sense. People often perceive Shah Rukh Khan as a series of works that make him a phenomenon! Actually, there are five or six quintessential films that makes the SRK dream – a phenomena! The list includes DDLJ, Kuch Kuch Hota Hai, Mohabbatein, Kal Ho Na Ho, Darr, and Baazigaar. There can be other choices also, but if you take a survey of people's favorite films of Shahrukh Khan, four out of these six films will always be there in most people's list. It is because the big records, huge popularity, and broad-spectrum mass hysteria these movies created that the image of a deathless lover or of passionate acting cannot be separated from Shah Rukh Khan!

Gradually, the phenomenon itself took over, and the popularity of the actor went beyond the popularity of just being a superstar, and this was because there is something in him—so strong and distinctive—that one can't simply walk away from. That unexplainable connection between Shah Rukh and the world makes them buy land on the moon and name exotic flowers after him. This inexplicable SRK fever went on for ages, earning him the biggest fan base on Earth. But more often, he behaves not like a star but with humility and conscience that set good examples for others. Amiability is one trait of Shah Rukh Khan that makes him such a big icon and people's favorite. He is therefore somebody who never any match, a peerless class altogether, someone who made us smile and cry – making us forget life's worries!

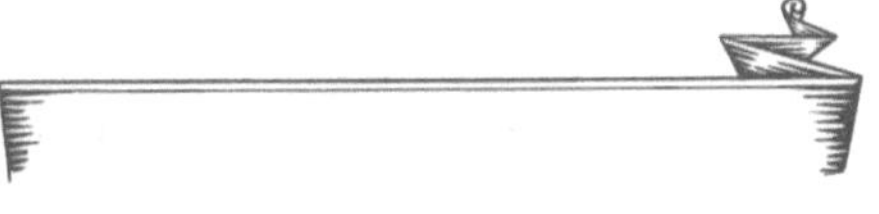

Chapter 5
Swades

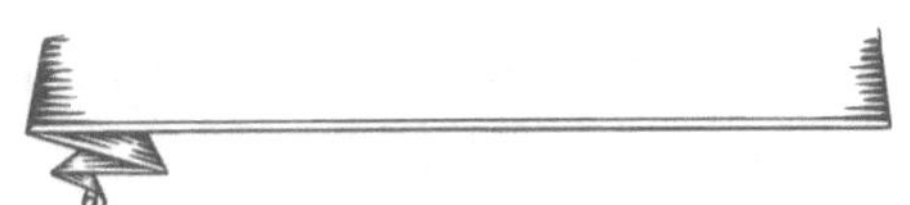

A film that has become a huge cult classic with passage of time is Swades which is also perhaps one of the finest Indian films ever made. Visioned and directed by Ashutosh Gowariker, the movie stars Shah Rukh Khan in a NASA scientist's role whose name is Mohan Bhargav. Unlike many patriotic films that border on chauvinism, Swades was the only one in a long time to showcase the tyranny that resides in the minds of our own Indian people and how people get trapped by their own evils!! The transparent and clear depiction of sociocultural scenario of India may have offended many at that time because many times, the truth, the bare truth, hurts!! But without knowing the truth, one cannot walk towards the path of redress as well!

AS SHOWN IN SWEDES, during Mohan's visit to India, he is completely perturbed by the socioeconomic scenario and the evils of caste system embedded in the soils of his own country. Shah Rukh Khan, as many would say, undid the 'known SRK' in this movie and gave a genuine, natural performance of the scientist who is forced to become a thinker and bringer of light in darkness of Indian superstitions! The conflicts and storms within the protagonist, the societal challenges and caste discrimination, the separation anxiety for being detached from his own country and the longing for a mother that he found in Kaveri Amma - could not be better played by anybody else other than Shah Rukh himself!

The star in SRK deglamorized himself to dive deep into the skin of Mohan Bhargava, the scientist who did not abandon his country because of his indifference of thoughts with local people. He did not abandon his country despite having a more comfortable life in the United States! While all the cast members of the film played their roles very well, it was Shah Rukh Khan who anchored and led the vision of Swades to immortal glory—something that engages everybody in their higher selves.

Swades is a film that forces you to think about the evil within the good and vice versa. Mohan and Gita force you to think about the generational limitations that can be countered only by education and enlightenment. Although the film did not do well at the box office, the film's destiny was written longer than its box office run; it was to become an indelible classic that showed India in all its truth and reality. Whether it was the condition of women or the lives of children who lives in the villages, whether it was the scarcity of water supply or the burning flames of social injustice - Swades showed us everything. Swades is a chapter in Indian cinema that will always be read and re-read critically, and the application of Shah Rukh Khan's acting technique was that of a maestro who found a way to control his genius, quite majestically!

Swades is the kind of film that you watch again and again to right the wrong and to bring about actual social changes instead of putting up justifications. It did not feel like a motion picture at all but reality in motion, and Shah Rukh's anchoring of the character Mohan Bhargava showed how much the country meant to him! He could have done another Main Hoon Na or K3G, earning loads of cash at the box office but the fact that the chose to do a film that would make a social difference – speaks volumes of his character. He and Asutosh Gowariker did it for society, although it took years for people to appreciate the real value of the film!

Swades is talked about and adored by Indians and foreigners till to this day, and it remains one of the most critically acclaimed Indian movies of all time. It also showed Ashutosh Gowariker as one of those few visionaries who can tap into the unknown territories of Shah Rukh Khan, making use of his gifts correctly. *Swades* marked the reaching of a cinematic maturity in the actor. And this meant there were many more masterpieces yet to come from the highly celebrated actor!

Chapter 6

Masterpieces

Although, with the overseas success of Kabhi Alvida Na Kehna and the success of Don, the actor had already become a megastar by the end of 2006, the best was yet to come. It happens with great actors that age makes them more and more artistically mature, thus making them more like the character than the self. There is a dissolution of reel and reality, and one cannot separate art from the artist! Although Shah Rukh has been doing this from a very early point in his career, which gave him the quick ladder to superstardom - it's the relentless pursuit of becoming better and better as an actor to serve humanity better that made the American dream of Shah Rukh possible! The success story of Shah Rukh Khan is one in a billion, and it is possibly the first time that a person from a middle-class, non-filmy background of India has reached such great global heights. It happened almost by accident, given that actor wanted to be a sportsperson but could not be, due to back injury.

HAVING ESTABLISHED himself as India's only megastar in a long time, it was Shah Rukh's time to show his mettle as an actor in the changing times of Gen-Next Indian cinema. It was a time when the audience choices were changing from watching good and time-worthy movies to knowing what the box office collection of that movie was. People become too concerned about box office numbers rather than content, genre or their own likeness for films. Previously before 2007-2008, people were not concerned about the box office numbers; they watched what they liked and did not what they disliked, and film watching should be as simple as that! However, post-2007, the focus of many shifted more to the box office than the content and performances in a film. People watched the films for box office numbers which is the wrong reason to watch any film. Fortunately, again, the rise of OTT platforms and web series in recent times reverted this focus back to the old trend of likeness-dislikeness-based, choice-based watching. In the Netflix era, there was a substantial normalization of this obsession with box office numbers and a reversal was made into good-old content-based movie watching.

It was the period between 2007 and 2010 when Shah Rukh Khan delivered some astounding performances that made him a timeless legend. Out of the deepest desire to pull something new out of the box, the actor went down the rabbit hole to do something novel, something that would justify his great success as an actor, something that would cement his legacy as a king in cinematic history! Three films were made by three extremely gifted directors of our generation who could harness the artistic oceaan of SRK. Two of them had already done films with Shah Rukh before: Aditya Chopra and Karan Johar, and the third director was new; his name is Shimit Amin. The films were Chak de India (2007), Rab ne Bana di Jodi (2008), and My Name Is Khan (2010). These three movies were very cinematically distinct from each other and very different from what Indian audiences were used to be seeing.

The coach of the Indian national women's hockey team

There are sensitive areas that celebrated stars do not venture into. They would think and rethink what it would do to their public image or to their future career. There are certain subjects that they would not even dare take up, like what happened in the case of Darr and Baazigar, an event that changed the history of Indian cinema and Shah Rukh Khan happened to India! Gradually, the world fell in love with the actor, giving him the status of king!!

It was in the year 2007 that a film by the actor was released, whose subject was Indian women's hockey team. Firstly, cricket is a very glorified sport in the country, and almost no other sport can match the craze and business of cricket in India. People would rather watch advertisements and endorsements done by cricketers than watch a hockey or football match played by their own nation. However, as in nowadays with the rapid burst of digitalization and with the start of different domestic sports tournaments in the country, Indian audiences are paying more attention to other games like hockey, kabaddi, and football – forget watching, it was not even a thought then! Here we are, talking about the pre-IPL generation when the best internet connectivity one could get was GPRS, or if one is very lucky, then 2G. Fast streaming of sports or media over the internet, and that too without any kind of buffering—was an only in imagination. These were the times when Facebook and Myspace were the social networking sites and single-screen cinemas were transforming into multiplexes.

It was Shah Rukh Khan who chose to make a very offbeat film in this era when smart communications and technology were at their cradle in the country. Another big problem was women's empowerment in sports, which still is but as the years pass, a larger section of people become aware of the country's social circumstances, there is a higher chance of at least some people acting in the right humanitarian manner to change its condition. India has a patriarchal society, and although the values of equality and social recognition of women have increased, women's empowerment remains an issue in larger parts of India – both rural and urban.

The same problem is reflected in the sports industry as well. Though cricket is a very popular sport in India, it mainly refers to the sport played by the men's cricket team, and not many audiences will switch on the television set to watch Indian women's cricket in those times.

Due to inadequate marketing and broadcasting of women sports, the audiences for women sports were very few those days. The film by Shimit Amin took on these serious issues of women empowerment in sports, sexism, funding politics and perceived discrimination. The film had the star presence of Shah Rukh Khan, the most-loved star in the country - to take the movie to the audiences. This was the second time in three years that Shah Rukh has attempted a serious role in a realistic film; the first being Swades, and now Chak de India.

The choice of these unconventional films also shows the psychology of a man who felt a certain responsibility towards talking about the real issues of the country in a time when doing patriotic films was not a line of business or a political stunt. As Shah Rukh Khan's commercial film success was huge and long-standing, the actor could have chosen to make two to three commercial movies per year that would make him richer, but no! through films he chose to speak up for India, his motherland! And the fact that he chose to do films taking on actual social issues, that too in those times when many actors will not even touch these sensitive subjects is what makes Shah Rukh Khan people's superstar, a courageous human being, and a true emperor!

He is a leader for good reasons and a pioneer of many things that were not done before. Actors do films that are often liked by audiences, such as family drama, patriotism, adultery, violence, overt heroism based on fallacy but nobody, neither the actors, directors, nor the Indian people, are ready to talk about the real problems that reside in the veins of the country. And this is what makes Chak de India special! Chak de India encompasses a range of themes like racial discrimination, differences in ethnic perceptions, communal prejudices, and equal opportunity. While the movie brilliantly captures the minute fragments and social cracks that live on in the communities of India, Shah Rukh Khan as the coach of the national women's hockey team, gives such an outstanding performance that it is revered to this day! Taking a sabbatical break from hockey after being alleged wrongly, the way Kabir

Khan returns to the scene as a coach and takes the national women's hockey team to World Cup win - is no less than a valiant achievement. The on-screen glory of women's hockey team in Chak De India led to the transformation of thoughts and practices in a real-world scenario and raised practical debates about the sporting future of India.

The movie inspired thousands of sportspersons and crores of Indians to fight for their rights and depicted how and why gender equality is important to bring collective success to a nation—not just ethically but socially and economically too. Not just women empowerment, the SRK movie showed us that if a wrong is done against you, you always get a chance to right it sometime, and when you get it, you must put in all your efforts to prove what mettle you are made up of! This is more so because it is your destiny that you are writing and there are only two stakeholders in it: you and God. The external factors (other people, society, dogmas, rules, laws, borders and divisions) are good only for a short period of time, but mostly, it is the inner force and courage to do things right, to stand up in the face of hardships— is what that becomes the greatest success stories of our lives! Correction, reformation, and the urge to right the wrong are moral forces, and it can be said that the actor here felt his moral duty towards a nation which gave him so much – in return, he gave us exceptional films like Swades and Chak de India!!

Chak de India captured the minute psychological and philosophical aspects of life, giving us a vital realisation about impermanence of life, about how both successes and failures are transient. And about the character Kabir Khan – SRK portrayed the minute phases of life changes, trauma, recovery, and transformation in such flawless manner that the movie became a big hit!

This movie also portrayed topics like social discrimination, negative stereotyping, classism, and the bigotry-attached issues that reside in the lanes and alleys of our country. Chak de India became a rage at that time, and people understood the serious cognitive, mental, and social underpinnings of bigger national problems such as women's subjugation, favoritism, gender inequality, and imperfect competition prevalent in the Indian sports industry. More importantly, Indian society saw a mainstream movie based on real-life modern-day issues, and the works of Shah Rukh Khan and other actors were highly appreciated. This earned Chak de India an unexpected box-office hit status, which the makers also had not foreseen. But the movie's sociocultural effect of Chak de India has always been beyond box-office records, just like the movie Swades.

Shah Rukh Khan is the only movie actor from the 90s generation who is so much loved, revered, and adored by people of all age groups, communities, and states of India. And this love allowed him to try films of different genres and take burning social topics to people which made him the face and brand ambassador of India.

Shah Rukh has unified India and its people many times. Whether through his cinematic presence or through humanitarian works, the actor made a wholesome difference to Indian society, reinstating its life-affirming values and film-loving nature! The love for Shah Rukh Khan defined the new rising India since the dawn of neoliberalism in 90s India. Because of the immense public support, Shah Rukh Khan was in an advantageous position playing the role of Kabir Khan because there is a deep likeness for the actor amongst the Indian masses (as one might think) but there was an equal risk of failure too. But it was the wisdom of Shah Rukh who decided to sign the film with the idea of playing it as it is, without tampering the shades of Kabir Khan's character. The actor, in the process, must have learned many things new, and for that, he had to unlearn many things - as goes the mechanics of human cognition. One does not have to be a die-hard fan to see how much SRK has transformed as an actor in Chak de India— he was someone who can control his consciousness, some who knows how to arch the bow according to the needs of the art, then throwing the arrow right! Right from Swades to Chak de India, Shah Rukh Khan developed this unique ability to synthesize unseen creativity that comes often late even in good actors, but in Shah Rukh, it came just at the right time of career! He became wiser in his choice of artistic output, which was to challenge the talent market of Indian directors and the perception of Indian masses in the coming years.

Chak de India was in many ways was Shah Rukh Khan's artistic culmination and awakening in a long time, since Kabhi ha Kabhi na or Dil se. In the latter, his character Amar passes through seven shades of love as mentioned in the Arabic literature - attraction, obsession, love, reverence, worship, obsession, and finaly, death. In many SRK films like Phir bi dil Hai Hindustani (2000), Josh (1999), Swades (2004), and Chak de India (2007), the reality of India has been shown in its bare bones and ribs, which makes Shah Rukh a great realistic actor as much as he is a big commercial filmstar!

The great actor dissected himself to become these characters, rather than dissecting the characters to fit himself. And that is what makes SRK films and roles so ionic that normal people strolling in the streets, children playing in the schoolyards, and elderly people from the old roofs of India can resonate with them, making SRK a name —bigger than anybody else—a feeling that assimilates thousand worlds into one! Shah Rukh Khan is indeed the best of two worlds who unifies audiences of different preferences and backgrounds, and this is more so because he is one of the most complete actors you will ever see in your life!

Films like Chak de India and Swades in many ways have inspired the thoughts behind national and social reforms in India. These films made clear statements about India's position in different areas like sports, education, poverty and diversity representation and SRK, as a citizen of India, made his voice clearly heard through these movies. Chak de India did move the wheel of change in India and made way for more socially focused films to be done in the future. Shah Rukh Khan has been an apolitical social leader for a long time, one who can set social trends and shape culture, and the film utilized his social leadership skills to portray the movie's protagonist in great way. Films like Chak de India are movies of a lifetime, and it will always be celebrated as one of the masterpieces of Shah Rukh Khan.

Rab ne Bana di Jodi—the extraordinariness of ordinariness

Rab ne Bana di Jodi was the first major Bollywood movie to release after the Mumbai terrorist attacks of 2008, and as one could remember, the film was released without any kind of promotions which was very unlikely, that too for a SRK film! This Aditya Chopra film was following up on the actor's last year's blockbuster, Om Shanti Om. The film saw Shah Rukh Khan playing a timid, middle-class, office-going person named Surinder Sahni. We were still in those times when box-office collections were not a big deal, but watching a nice, honest, and feel-good movie was. People still had their own opinions in those days and were not swayed by the amateur discussions as on the internet forums today. Although the Internet has been useful in many ways, it has also been unnecessarily overhasty and injudicious at times. It was the single-screen era, and people use to storm the streets and main roads, blocking cars and buses, despite fever and sickness - to watch SRK in the movie theatres —a feat yet to be achieved by many other actors! Rab ne Bana di Jodi, despite the lack of promotions and media hype, saw a huge crowd even in the fearful times of terrorism! The driving factor was easy - Shah Rukh Khan, India's heartbeat!!

The actor once again showed that love is bigger than hatred, and he is the man who will keep on showing you that for a lifetime! A simple story set in the streets of Punjab depicts the life of an ordinary man who does the daily chores himself and works at a nearby office. He is then married to a girl whose love interest has died accidentally. The girl does not desire him, but deep inside, his affection for the girl waves — the girl who is already his wife! The movie was an antithesis of Dilwale Dulhania Le Jayenge, made by the same director-actor combination: Aditya Chopra and Shah Rukh Khan. While Dilwale Dulhania Le Jayenge took us on the inspiring ride of a prince charming who crossed borders and frontiers to finally reach his destined lover, Rab Ne Bana Di Jodi contrastingly took us deep into the reality of India's marriage culture!

The movie was based on several themes: the age difference between the husband and wife, middle-class family norms and their daily ongoings, an awkward silence and the anticipations of two people who have been thrown into a strange bond of togetherness called marriage.

The plain environment and unembellished scenes of the movie—the silent encounters between two newly married people who have been diced together by hands of fate—gave it a tone of striking sincerity that reflected lives in many middle-class families in India, no matter which state or what sect! With conversations beginning between the couple, with the wife taking care of the solitary man - affection and warmth bloomed inside the husband for his wife which, he confesses to his best friend Bobby running a saloon in the locality. And that must be one of the scenes when, in front of a mirror, SRK's character Surinder Sahni gives one of the most enthralling monologues ever - where he reflects upon himself and the possible desires of a young woman such as his wife. His reflection is imbued with such sincerity and honesty that it could have even moved mountains!! The self-confession of his love for his own wife—that he wants to be returned by her too, not by force but by earning it—sent waves of warmth and heartache to a million people who watched the film!!

This was another occasion when Shahrukh captured unknown territories of his own artistic genius and made the movie's journey possible for us. He made the story of Surinder Sahni possible for the audiences, for the cynics, for the optimists and the pessimists, for the believers and also for the givers who must have felt what Suri went through! However, out of this crisis, to make it special for his wife, he imagined what she must be wanting in a man— and the character of Raj was born! Raj is meant to be an overly energetic, highly enthusiastic and very outspoken kind of guy who wear 'macho' type jeans and flashy dresses with forever changing sunglasses to look 'cool'—a character also played by Shah Rukh Khan himself. Although this was the main twist of the movie, the dynamics of inner and outer experiences of life built upon the most interesting segments of the movie—the one in which Raj and Taani have a 'Golgappa competition' and then when Surinder eats *biryani* made by his beloved wife; the other in which Surinder approves the request of his wife to take part in a dancing competition and gives her the money almost without exchanging a word and then smiles shyly when she thanks him—are the spirituals that make Rab Ne Bana Di Jodi special! The little moments of happiness and sadness were so well portrayed by Shah Rukh Khan, especially in the character of Surinder, that they would keep you on your feet throughout the run of the movie. And the fact that the emotions of the character Surinder were naturally muffled and masked, given his personality, and hardly did he express anything in front of his wife but trying to do things that would make her happy - is made Surinder Sahni the most endearing person you will ever see!

Surinder is about humanity, compassion, and truthfulness. And the earnest embodiment of Surinder by Shah Rukh made Rabe ne Bana di Jodi – a great, great film! There was something about the character Surinder Sahni that, whenever he was expressing himself (to himself or to the audience) or to his wife (as after the sumo fight), the tone and pitch of the character, the use of a characteristically reserved voice, and that faithful shakiness whenever his wife comes to talk to him - stimulated our higher selves to become kinder and more compassionate to ourselves and others around us! Nobody but Shah Rukh Khan can dissolve the borders between reality and movies, and he can inspire you to change as a human being. The character Raj, on the other hand, did everything that can be done in a film—the filmy dance sequences, the smoldering hero dialogues, the wooing of a girl in grand style of festivities and colors! And the character Raj is so characteristically different, almost like an antithesis of Surinder Sahni, that you almost forget that it is played by the same man, Shah Rukh Khan.

While the personality of Surinder was very shy and understanding, the persona of Raj was extroversive, outgoing, and that of a restless man who can go any lengths to impress a girl! Surinder was the man playing the character Raj, and he was the one stretching himself, changing himself completely, to become Raj but a great deal of agony and longing made him do so! So, in a way, what Raj could do could be done by Surinder, but what Surinder could do, only Surinder could do!! And this was all to get the affection from a person he actually cares about—his own wife! The way SRK played both characters with absolute demarcation in terms of body language, voice and style shows the versatility of an actor who has could captivate people of the world with his extraordinary gifts!

What was there in the movie? An old, broken house? the local streets and changing of seasons? a salon, a garage, and an auditorium?! Now the question is: What was filmy about the film Rab Ne Bana di Jodi? may be just the character of Raj and just the two songs which portrayed just one thing - Surinder's perception of Taani's likeness for a filmy, hero-like life partner. Despite being told Raj and Surinder is the same person, may will still believe that they are two different persons became they are seeing Raj and Surinder as two very distinct people in the movie. Many would even feel, especially towards the climax of the movie, that both Surinder and Raj are almost competing against each other for the love of same girl! To one, she is sort of a friend-girlfriend person, and to another, she is his wife!! This is more so because the characteristic difference has been projected in your head; the demarcation has already been created! You just cannot differentiate reality from the illusion being created on the screen—the illusion of Raj and Surinder being two different persons, although deep down, you know they are the same!

But you just can't help the feeling. You cannot help but feel a certain degree of distinctive difference between these two characters, you cannot help thinking they are both different, very different, two distinct human beings, each having their own separate lives and values! And such was the superlative craftmanship of the actor Shah Rukh Khan, a man who cannot die!! The magic SRK does—the captivation he gets you into—is one of a kind realm all together, and there is no parallel that exists to this master-actor! One might say or think, how could a person not identify the same person who was once wearing glasses and once not? Who was once having a moustache and once not? And anybody who is thinking this is thinking because you know who Shah Rukh Khan is, you know how he looks, and you have strong familiarity with his appearance and image created over the years. And if you ever had this thought, that indicates you have pulled into a deeper deception! This is because everybody knows the actor very well, and the fact that he has been shown to be changing from one character to another might just give one the idea - of how somebody cannot see the resemblance?! but that's not what you generally feel during the movie. You might feel it after the movie may but during the movie, you are flying deeper into the story of Raj, Taani and Surinder! Or should we say Surinder and his wistful struggle to make his wife happy?!

During the movie, you have already developed the idea in your mind that two characters are different in the way they appear and present themselves, and most people will not think about the resemblance at all because they are more concerned with: what will happen to Suri at last, or will Raj take Taani away? Such is the art of the movie! It is all very simple, but still, it gets you every time you watch it!! There is no complexity in the screenplay, no usage of very expensive props or tools as such, but it is the great acting of the greatest actor of our generation that made Surinder Sahni and Rab Ne Bana Di Jodi a triumph of love and culture! The film taught us about friendship (the one that existed between Surinder and Bobby and the one that existed between Raj and Taani); it taught us about developing a sense of understanding, friendship, and life-like bonding that should practically be possible between every married couple (as depicted between Surinder and Taani).

RNBDJ taught us if you want, you can be considerate and kind towards other people, towards your partner, and also towards yourself; and nobody can change you if you do not want to change!!

The film gave us various life lessons on a very mature note, and the movie indeed had a very deep effect on minds and souls of the middle-class, married, and non-married Indian people who go through similar dynamics of mixed emotions, waiting and sufferings !

The statement was not only for the people who had or were about to have arranged marriage but for the whole institution of marriage! In the bigger picture, Rab ne Bana Di Jodi revolutionized the concept of a hero – teaching us that there exists a hero in all of us and also that the good guys don't always finish last, indeed! Taani's choice for her silent and sober husband over an ideal lover-boy guy showed us that good can be returned with good, and at the end, it is only your karma that matters! Surinder was good to her from the beginning, and good happened back to him despite all the pain he had to go through! Surinder was a man who lived calmly in solitude and he was kind enough to marry a girl who did not desire him! He married her without knowing what his future would be!! He fell for her, not knowing she would ever love him back or not?! and he decided to even lose his identity to make the girl happy who loves him not! Despite everything, the silence and kindness of Surinder triumphed at the end, making him his wife's only hero!! I don't know about others but I have not watched a more beautiful love story than Rab ne!

The movie is a great lesson to the entire world that good people and good relationships do exist, and there are multiple reasons to believe in them. Rab ne Bana di Jodi gave us the perfect reformation on the Indian culture of marriage and what men should be like and how women should be treated, inside and outside marriage. It should also be true the other way around: a wife should also be kind to her husband, and there should be mutual understanding, as Rahul Khanna has quoted 'Pyar dosti hai! Love is friendship.'

Being kind to each other is an essence of humanity; at least being kind to the people who have tied their lives to you is more than important! And Surinder Sahni remains the best representation of a holy soul, of endurance, and of true kindness that can ever be!

My name is Khan – thoughts

The portrayal of Rizwan Khan by Shah Rukh in the 2010 movie 'My name is Khan' that takes on strenuous subjects of terrorism, antisemitic perceptions, religious prejudices and intolerance is perhaps the most critically appreciative work and magnum opus of Shah Rukh Khan. The secular attitude of the actor has always been the highlight since a long time - whether it is in the choice of his movies, or attending social events or his worshipping of many gods of different religions at home and outside that makes him more of a spiritual person than a religious one. And these intrinsic values might have given the actor the right reason to play the role of Rizwan - whose ideals are also similar: tolerance, secularity, and equality! Rizwan Khan gave a great opportunity to SRK to speak the same language on which his life and filmography are based—the same words of spirituality, tolerance, love, and humanism. And the ideas about humanity and peace do remain more or less the same for every human, and these do not change based on the environment one lives in or based on the experiences one has during a lifetime until they are traumatic or very unjustified. Still, people do take the path of peace, the road that unites us with God!

The ideas of benevolence and mutual understanding are fundamental, and there is no deviation possible where the meanings of peace or humanity could change to violence or intolerance!! Thus, if anybody think of committing acts of terrorism, coercion, extortion, or any other form of criminal activity on other communities who are humans just like the rest of us, as good as bad, as sad as happy as all other people of different beliefs - then it is certainly the most uncivilized thought ever to reside in a human mind!! It is indeed the most uneducated and loutish idea ever that makes one believe that some religion, some country, or some people who have a certain religious faith or an alternative lifestyle are not human, and this shows how much hostility reside in the minds of human beings - people who would not think of other people as people! While the irony is - human beings are believed to be human beings because they can think, they can leash their animal spirits to be kind souls – but in truth, many are far from attaining the human state – people who could not free themselves from shackles of rudimentary thoughts to inhibit themselves from doing the wrong! These are the people who are ought to be awakened by the widely available tools of education and faculties of rationality available in the 21st century because they are not yet. It is the fallacious attributing of each other to acts of sin, and the cold, unjust bitterness that we seed for each other breeds the spirit of evil and gives birth to terrorism!! But how long can we allow this to happen? God or religion has nothing to do with instilling violence just like prejudices, stereotypes, terror and hostility-fed separatist attitudes have nothing to do with God or compassion!! For some people, terrorism is a choice—a choice that gives rise to the ungodly and inhuman religion of terrorism. There is no God nor human in terrorism, only evils, devils, and demons changing claws!

The protagonist of the movie MNIK becomes a sufferer of this unjust prejudice, bearer of this unjust inhuman attribution of evil to a religion. This fallacious attribution happens to Rizwan to such an extent that civilized people of civilized worlds and even his own family members mistreat him! The discrimination suffered at every juncture of life, the sufferings caused by detachment from his wife, the death of a young son and social struggles of autism take the protagonist on a journey of self-search! The journey of Rizwan was the journey to truth and oneness, the journey of a right-thinking man against the evils of terror to correct the collective wrong of humankind. Rizwan Khan is a performance of coruscating radiance from the ever-thoughtful actor that inhabits in Shah Rukh Khan. Coming to the acting part, the stereotyping of movements, the constant usage of the same words, the bursts of impulsivity and sudden bursts of apprehension with episodic anxiety that led his loneliness and social isolation – made a great depiction of a Asperger's individual who runs into loneliness and distrust due to his religion! The technicality and brilliance of the actor were on display in the extraordinary journey of Khan: 'Khan from the epiglottis'. The stretching of human kindness is akin to godliness, and this becomes the main crux of protagonist's persona in the movie. Sometimes, the character conflicts with his clinical bearings of Asperger's syndrome (such as anxiety or social isolation), sometimes with the pain of life, sometimes with the color yellow! It is the battle within and the battle outside Rizwan that make the character so singular, a character who battle made battle from within! The character's mighty, thought-provoking response to sheer injustice of the world in the long journey he takes, is a principal lesson on the exercise of humanistic powers and a testimony on practice of conscience!!

To discuss the actor's commitment, the preparation for such a distinguished role who experiences conflict, isolation, discrimination and pain in the journey of truth takes nothing less than an unworldly flair in a person to shine in it! And as many would say, only the actor Shah Rukh Khan has it—that one extra mile that makes him exceptionally remarkable.

Chapter 7

Achieving global stardom and an experimental decade

By the year 2011, SRK had already become the world's biggest star, a status affirmed by biggest media platforms and people of the world. There cannot be any debate about the aura and effect of Shah Rukh Khan who always has won love of the people. Although, due to the successful international shows and constant appreciation of his films by audiences and film-societies worldwide, Shah Rukh Khan already had a global name; achieving the title 'World's Biggest Movie Star' meant he was officially one - and the only one in the history of Indian cinema to reach there! This should not come as a shock to anybody, as the man has been the face of Indian cinema since the 90s. Shah Rukh can romance, beat up villains, be a villain, dance, emote, make you laugh, give you tears and manifest love - near-complete actor who has a own golden arcade of popular movies made people fall in love with him again and again!

In fact, many international markets opened up by massive success of Shah Rukh Khan films worldwide, other Indian actors and filmmakers could release their films there and earn from there! The amount of love, reverence, and unbeatable fandom that SRK received are because of the prayers which people pray for him, wishing him luck and seeing his success as their theirs! Shah Rukh Khan is love and love is Shah Rukh Khan – time and time, he has come and freed us from beads of monotony and hatred – making our lives colorful and our hearts strong! if he will not have that unmatched stardom, when who will? He gave

Indian cinema and Indian people, people from around the world so much !! if he will not have the gold crown then who will?

The earning of the Ordre des Arts et des Lettres (2007) and Lé gion d'honneur (2014) from the French government; L'Etoile d'Or (2011) from the government of Morocco; and the Brand Laureate Legendary Award (2012) from the government of Malaysia, sealed his world's biggest movie star status. This also meant if the actor was India's biggest movie actor before 2010, post 2010 he became the world's biggest star, meaning many people from different parts of the world did connect to the phenomenon that is SRK. He is a man whose stardom extends to a legion of countries, especially in larger segments of Europe, almost all of the Middle Eastern countries, Africa, Australia, Malaysia and others. He is a man whose artistic works have been recognized and appreciated by people from all over the globe, and even in small villages in Africa, they play Shah Rukh songs!

The actor has received major awards and recognition from six out of seven continents of the world. So, around 2011–2012, Shah Rukh Khan is not just an Indian megastar but a globally recognized actor whose works are celebrated all over the globe in cities and towns and in far-disconnected places, making him a living legend and a prodigal cinematic success!

Now, just to think about what the psychology of a man would be—the one who is at the pinnacle of everything? He must feel himself as God, but this is where the difference lies! Shah Rukh Khan respects the power and love he received and he remains humble about it. He never used his gifts and powers wrongly that most people will, if given they are given his position! He was God's child then; he is God's child now, and even after achieving things that nobody could possibly ever achieve, he remains as humble as ever, never forgetting the moments of struggle that took him to the throne! And this is where Shah Rukh Khan remains one gem of a human being who is as kind, as compassionate, as a King with blessings of God should be!! He is an inspiration for billions of people who have known his struggles to the last soaring pillar where he stands now! He stands now at the highest rock where he represents us – his friends! his fans! his believers!! Think, what is the need of a person of his stature to make movies any further? He might choose not to because what he has achieved and found in life is a perfect American dream! In a way, his life is a living dream and what else could he possibly want from it? But it is that drive to keep acting that keeps the man going, and he keeps doing the movies to make his fans and audience happy, not for any box-office numbers on the chart! And this attitude of Shah Rukh Khan: despite having a gifted charm and immense artistic talent that earned him so much success, he chooses to go on making films for people to be happy!!

SRK is big-hearted and compassionate human being - he gives importance to other people, he listens to others! The actor always puts equal amount of enthusiasm in everything he does, and this is an important life lesson for success – to put your heart in what you want to achieve! He feels when somebody speaks to him, whether it is a fan, a reporter, another fellow actor or a neutral audience and these relentless acts of generosity from the man who has seen it all - makes him the King of hearts. He keeps attending the public events, the corporate meetings, and the national seminars, never leaving a moment to acknowledge his fans and the people who made him a star! This is to reiterate that he is a man who never had competition because people like Shah Rukh Khan, who is adored by billions of people beyond the boundaries of caste, creed, religion and society should not be compared; instead, they should be taken as good examples! You don't compare Gods; you should not compare good people! Comparing good with good leads to bad!

Now, if he is taking on the challenges of bringing new concepts of moviemaking or commercializing VFX to tell the stories of India, should we, not his fans and his well-wishers, support him in this venture? If Shah Rukh is thinking of the country's cinematic procced despite some of his recent failures, then should not we see him as a visionary leading from the front?! If he is doing these for the progress of the country on the technological or cinematic front, then it is something that makes Shah Rukh Khan a leader and visionary in his own right, and isn't it something we should be proud of? That a person with such massive influence is not tearing up society and trying to unite the world of cinema? It also justifies the fact that he made experimental movies like Ra-One, Fan, or Zero that were too ahead of their time. Yes, the storytelling was flawed in Zero and the storyline was weak in Ra-One, but the essence of both movies were different; they are to be watched for the newness and years of hard work that every member of those films have put in to make the exceptional cinematic experience possible for us! And this goes not only for movies but for any field of work where people have genuinely worked hard and deserve appreciation for it. Even if one cannot appreciate, there is no reason to spread hatred against a person who has been the face of our cinema and representative of crores of countrymen! Whether it is Fan, Zero, or Ra-one, one can watch them for the novelty factor, or it can also be watched for the man who has given us decades of great memories that we can possibly not forget ever in our lifetimes! People like Shah Rukh Khan are the reason why people unite; they are the glue which hold society together! Shah Rukh Khan reeks of good vibes and true leadership qualities that brings people together in bands of culture, togetherness and friendship! And life would be incomplete without mentioning him!!

Human beings like continuity and things that have been constant against struggles and times for a long period of time are perceived as examples of success! The Shah Rukh phenomenon has been a constant thing for a very long stretch of time, hence another reason why people look up to him as a good role-model! Human cognition is shaped by various types of patterning like connectedness, closure, continuity, similarity, and proximity (the five gestalt principles). The movies and journey of Shah Rukh Khan are amongst the special things that people connect and find continuity with - hence people relate to the man, his struggles, and his finding of reverent success despite having come from a middle-class family! Shah Rukh Khan has indeed given us a star-band of magnificent films, but beyond that, there is also a lot of collective human psychology that drives his star phenomenon beyond Bollywood and cinema!

There are a lot of chronological, historical, and cultural factors that make the SRK a sensation - fitting the archetype of a king. If globalization and liberalization trends helped build the initial stardom of Shahrukh, it was the universal social acceptance and hard dedication of Shah Rukh that made his fairy tale possible in the later parts! So many generations, so many different people of different nations cannot keep liking one actor decade and decade if something special is not involved! You might not like SRK; you might not even like his films, but his passion, commitment, and honesty with the acting part is something you cannot deny! There is a lot of hard work, passion and sacrifice involved in whatever he created, he endured a lot in what he became a star! Do you think a man who has shaped the culture and values of a country and inspired dreams in billions of people across the world—a receiver of global stardom—will possibly be swayed by some mere box office hiccups?

SRK is a man who is the force of nature, a sheer tour de force who cannot be overtaken because he has lived it all—the beginnings and the endings, the highs and the lows—and he is now at the pinnacle of his artistic maturity. From the movie 'Fan' (an exemplary of craftsmanship) to the movie 'Zero', the actor is taking up new ways of moviemaking and storytelling. A lot of courage and risk-taking were displayed by the actor, which he did for the sake of art and evolution. In the words of Ralph Waldo Walder, 'The more the experiments, the better', and the fact that the actor keeps trying and trying without giving up is what makes him a champion. The fact that he keeps trying even after achieving everything is one of his brightest attributes that grants him the respect and love of others! Nobody can ever possibly think of doing a gray character like Gaurav Channa (in Fan) or a vertically challenged Bauah Singh (in Zero) if it is not Shah Rukh Khan; only he has that extra dimension, that extra courage to go that extra mile! Fan failed at the box office, but he still made Zero - so, one cannot help but applaud the courageous attempts taken by the great actor to bring novelty into the Indian cinema. Now, see what has happened? Everything has changed with Pathaan and Jawan. It is this very unfaltering determination that made Shah Rukh Khan Shah Rukh Khan - an emperor!

One of the reasons why no one can take the place of Shah Rukh Khan is because the place is heart and there are too many filmy things and memories of life attached to the phenomenon that is Shah Rukh Khan. He has taught you too many things; his films have been your friend in good and bad times, and he has made you happy on so many occasions. As a fan, as a follower, or even as a general audience with some intellect, you can allow SRK's experimentation to happen; you can let the complex arts take their roots. And it is also a matter of happiness for all of us that the actor has taken up the hard life of an artist to transcend human consciousness rather than making only phoney, meretricious movies that will fare at the box office. The fact that he is realising, accepting, and harmonising the need for groundbreaking works to teach and bring novel ideas to the younger generation is what makes Shah Rukh Khan a thoughtful person and social thinker.

Whether it is the apperceptive nature or disturbing composure of the obsessed fan Gaurav in 'Fan' movie or the impulsive nature of character Bauah Singh in 'Zero', it always keeps you guessing and thinking. And you can do nothing but appreciate the range of characters that the man can play onscreen with such veracity and finesse! These latest movies of the actor from the last decade may not leave you in exalting joy (like it did in *Om shanti Om* or *Main Hoon Na*) or in a great sadness (like we were in *Dil se* or *Devdas),* but one thing is for sure: one will still be captivated by the uncanny artistic abilities of the most gifted actor of our generation, Shah Rukh Khan. Hitting one at a sensitive spot (patriotism, good versus evil, etc.) to earn box office numbers is convenient, but taking audiences into the new dimension of art is difficult. Difficult but true, that's one of the fundamental functions of art—creativity.

In the last decade, from 2010 to 2020, there has been a lot of experimentation by the ageing actor, a lot of trial and error where he is applying the wisdom learned from years of acting and filmmaking into the creation of something new - which do take a lot of courage. From being called upon to give speeches at international universities to being bestowed with so many international accolades, the global success of Shah Rukh Khan has surged by leaps and bounds in the last decade. People of known and unknown nationalities screamed and broke barricades to see their all-time favorite hero, Shah Rukh Khan, and if the scenes outside Mannat was breathtaking on the actor's birthday, then the public reception of the actor in foreign lands was flabbergasting as well!

You can apply Maslow's pyramid to describe his situation. Shah Rukh Khan has achieved too much glory in a very short period, and because all of his other social and belonging needs are met, the actor feels the need to experiment and dissect himself; he feels the need to self-actualize. So many times, one may have seen this with great men and women; they are always in an existential search for a meaning in life, and so is the actor's case.

He is the man of the masses; he is the lifeblood of a nation, its people, and its generations; and he will always keep doing everything that would make the nation happy. That is why, despite having such a royal stardom where one can easily think of him acting in a Hollywood movie, he does not want to! It has to be Shah Rukh Khan who thinks for the people still, the people of his country who made him a star in the first place. The intensity of experimentation has been so strong in the movie 'Fan' that it makes the audience echo the emotions and feelings that propel the life force of his magical fandom! It is great to see the actor taking on sensitive topics like fandom and stardom, obsession, and the psychological toil of being an idol or a worshipper. Every fan of every movie actor can relate to the facts that were shown in the movie, and it is true that any fandom or worship of any god by any humans cannot come alive without some form of obsession. Now, how much that obsession is growing into compulsion—how much that compulsion is growing into uncontrollable actions to prove the compulsions correct and to fit the lengths of one's obsession—is something that one needs to observe and keep in check. Obsession is different from dedication, and to be a dedicated fan is different from being an obsessed fan—a subject very well portrayed in the movie Fan.

The movie 'Fan' took on such a strenuous subject which is appropriate for an actor of his caliber—someone who has an enviable world-level fan following to justify the subject of the movie. Moreover, the movie also showed the reality of people who cannot control themselves when their demands are not fulfilled. Most of the followers and majority of the fans will be loyal to their favorite actors and advocate for their idol for a very long period of time, and for some, that advocacy might encompass a lifetime where a fan becomes a devotee. This would mean an unconditional attachment to their idol that cannot be rationalized by logical thoughts—something that describes the stardom of SRK nicely —people love him, respect him, and even worship him because they see God's hand reaching out to Shah Rukh Khan.

Sometimes you protect your ideas and attachments so much that they become obsessions, but yes, again, obsession is different from dedication! The cause is the meaning that attached you to an idea in the first place; it's general psychology; it's Freud's theory of unconsciousness! There is an association!! You see The Shah Rukh idea, the globalization idea, and the idea of Sachin Tendulkar as the best batman are the concepts that people of 90s generation grew up with, and hence, as they are embodied in their unconscious, they will knowingly or unknowingly shield those ideas! It is also true that people turn revengeful and violent because their definitions of what's good have not been met and their definitions of what's right have not been done. This happens to all of us at some stage of life, and given the age of 'Gaurav Channa' in the movie 'Fan', one cannot expect maturity. But if one looks at the other side of the picture, it was the longing of the fan to meet his favourite hero, and it is true only that because of people's love only, stardom became possible, so, the film meets both sides of the picture.

Shah Rukh Khan has lifelong followers and devotees, and it is justifiable for him to do the movie 'Fan', but to nail both the characters of Aryan Khanna and Gaurav with such acuity and sharpness that bends the fabric of reality - to make it almost surreal, can only inspire you to become a Shah Rukh fan once more! The chase sequence in the film and scenes when the actor hurts his own wax statue or breaks the glass of his own photo frame show how much the actor could empathize with the feelings of others, especially those of fans. First comes fandom, then comes stardom, and the gigantic fandom has almost become an extension of the actor's identity in the last thirty years.

As they say, there is a fear of the unknown. In the words of psychology, xenophobia is something that this actor's experimentalism takes you to. Sometimes, it can be a happy experience; sometimes, it can be a sad one, but sometimes it can be a nerve-racking and enthralling one too. Shah Rukh is a self-actualizing man who is honing up his craft in ways unknown, but the man is becoming only better as a self-knowing actor with the usage of experimentalism as his acting philosophy. People still ask the actor to do 'Chaiya Chaiya' or to say a dialogue from an old movie that they are so fond of, and this shows how much the actor's works have affected people!! Most of the actor's films are immortal and evergreen, given the massive popularity they have amongst the masses, and their impact has reached far-reaching lands to change values and perceptions of human beings!! If this is true, then it is also true that people are already stuck with the image of Shah Rukh Khan that is of 'an undying lover! And they search for something related to that in every film of his!! It is again that compulsive need to fill the pattern, to live the holism.

Now, when he is making new films that are very different from what has been done before, there comes a moment of conflict when you are trying to witness the well-known actor in a different way, but the flashes of old SRK movies come to your mind!! But at the same time, one's consciousness is also broadened when one is seeing new things, reciting new ideas, and coming in touch with creativity. You can almost feel it in your veins—a rapid maturing of the actor, the development of the arts, and the soulful drive of a man—retained in SRK even after decades of colossal success. And that's how the process of ageing works: the more you age, the more you understand the value of life and the more you let of things without having to lose yourself.

Chapter 8

THE STAR, THE CELEBRATION

And growing up of a country

Shah Rukh Khan fever first hit the country when the winds of neo-liberalization started and gale of globalization took over India, thus allowing a fast exchange of international cultures. India is a land of many cultures and religions, and constitutionally, it is secular and democratic. Therefore, a lot of opinions, rights, and notions shape the national picture from time to time. There are millions of people walking the roads, hundreds of films made every years, hundreds of deities worshipped, and thousands of prayers prayed every day. There are vast forestlands and high mountains; there are plains and plateaus; there are temples and mosques; there are gurudwaras; and there are those beautiful churches in India which holds serene peace. Two things are common in all of these places: human beings and beatings in their hearts, in the name of Shah Rukh Khan. If one name is synonymous with the name of the country, that name is of Shah Rukh Khan. Whether it is the vast assemblage of people outside his house on this birthday or the running people chasing his car in every part of the country the actor travels, there is always an unfathomable love - as if someone from their family has arrived!

They chant his name while carrying his posters and placards, which proves Shah Rukh is somebody who means so much to common people. It is not only about box office records or winning awards but also the connection he has—the silver cord between him and the world, which is most powerful. He is a social leader, a movie phenomenon who motivates people to take up the path of their dreams. And he is also the one who redistributes rights back to the people. Whether through memorable films or through important social works, he has made people realize what their rights are and why they should never give them up. The actor has always been straightforward about his actions, and this is a life lesson for everybody: if one is determined about his or her goals and have a diligent pursuit towards achieving them, then the goals can be achieved one day! His legacy extends to people who watched his movies day and night, days after days, for years and decades, so much that there is a projection of him in them, and they are the ones who make the stardom and the myth of SRK possible! There is a Shah Rukh Khan in everybody because he describes and inscribes the feeling of love with and this is where the actor becomes a country's identity, the face of generations—a legacy that will be remembered for a long time!

You will hardly find anybody who has not watched Dilwale Dulhania Le Jayenge or Kuch Kuch Hota Hai and it is even more impossible to find somebody who has not tried the actor's famous pose or said the actor's dialogues ever in their life. Boys and girls, mothers and grandmothers, men and grandfathers—everybody likes Shah Rukh Khan to a point of adornment, and there is a special spot for the super-actor in mostly everybody's lives. The fact that he has played diverse characters that broke the barriers of religions, roles, and values—a lover, a villain, a soldier, a patriot, a teacher, a student, a husband, a psychopath, a star, a fan, and many more— that he became a rage, a ray of Love! SRK has a fandom, aura and stardom like no other, his movies created big records at the box office many many times and sometimes they could not, but the fact that his movies and humanitarian actions overall have had a big impact on the social, economic and cultural scenario of India is what makes the 'SRK phenomenon' a driving force of India's rise.

While movies like Dilwale Dulhania Le Jayenge, Dil Toh Pagal Hai, Kuch Kuch Hota Hai, Mohabattein, and Veer Zaara taught us the truest meaning of friendships and love; his movies like Swades, Pardes, Phir Bhi Dil Hai Hindustani, and Chak de India gave India the impetus to change its cultural and social values in fighting of injustice. If Rab Ne Bana di Jodi taught people to respect and be kind to their husbands and wives, My Name is Khan taught the world to be kind to each other because, at the end, we all bleed blood—the same red blood cells. It is important not to ever forget what we share as humans, and from the cognizance of this similarity, the spirit of compassion can be evoked! Not to forget how the versatile actor has made a joke of himself to make everybody laugh, as in Yes Boss, Duplicate, or in first half of Zero, and the heartbreak he gave us in Kal ho na Ho—there is something in Shah Rukh Khan that lives on and will be transferred from generations to generations to keep alive the phenomenon that he will be always!

Shah Rukh Khan is a happy accident whose name flutter waves in a million hearts and flickers the memories brightest, and that is because the actor's movies or presence is not restricted to the 70 mm silver screen, but they flow out of it to have an impact on the colors of people's lives!! This makes the SRK phenomenon omnipresent, especially in India. His movies have changed everything around in India, from how people think of relationships, of cinemas, and of essential aspects of life to its meaning and purpose. The aura so luminous in Shah Rukh Khan has redefined the meanings of happiness or sadness that we laugh and cry watching his movies, still after thirty years. The charm of SRK's screen presence is so riveting that it makes people unify with the messages, philosophies, and notions depicted in his films!

SRK movies bring transformations in individual lives and shifts at the societal level. SRK films transcend space and time to inspire the social sphere on earth, and very few men and women have had these leadership qualities that shaped the history of the world. Yes, a film can make you happy, a film can entertain you, and yes, a film can even preach, but films in general cannot transcend or transform you until they have the lifelike aura of actors like Shah Rukh Khan. Not just films, but any work, any life, any story cannot come to life if it does not have the soul of that one person who is going through it every day, and SRK- actor lives the character of his films—with such dedication and passion that makes us more like him!

Even if a movie is far from reality, there is something in each of the Shah Rukh Khan films that makes you want at least some parts of your life to be like that, and there comes the need for a change. In general, human behavior is generally shaped by actions that they think are more evolved, and this shaping comes either from the inside (through one's own experiences or insight) or from the outside (through observational or vicarious learning). Both are true, and both mechanisms influence the change process. And this is another critical reason behind the actor being a great social leader: he is a good role model, shaping people's lives through his work.

Good things and good people give you the courage to change for the better. And this is where Shah Rukh Khan is a man who inspires people from all generations and all backgrounds, and even in places where people do not have television or a smartphone, they know of the legend. Shah Rukh Khan often talks of unification and collaboration and not of separation and withdrawal—creating movies to unify India! There exists a wireless connection between the loved actor and the people of India, where people wait for his films even for four or five years. People of hundreds of nationalities bond in front of Mannat, as the name of Shah Rukh Khan echoes with the name of love, friendship!

The symbol in Shah Rukh Khan drove institutional changes in the dogmas of social relationships. And the society and social values of India, driven by its vigorous film culture, have become more based on liberalism and friendship largely due to the movies of Shah Rukh. He, who represented the new, liberal India. There have been several companies since the 1990s, both multinational and Indian, who have used the actor's aura and stardom to make a market for their products in the country. And if the companies have established themselves in India due to the face value of Shah Rukh Khan, then one will have to say that the actor has impacted not only the social or cultural upliftment of the country but also its economic prosperity. One can notice that SRK has been the face of companies and corporations from different industries, and if they have established themselves from nobody to somebody in the country's business environment, then a vital part of their establishment can be attributed to the 'SRK phenomenon'.

If this is true, then the offices and branches they expanded upon, the hiring and recruitment they did - have increased employment in the country, and indeed, there is a major hand in this SRK phenomenon which drove this socio-economic progress. Hence, the gradual attainment of golden stardom by Shah Rukh has not only been a treat to his fans or a source of the actor's increasing net worth but it has also realistically helped India to grow economically and socially with great momentum. The 'SRK phenomenon' can be explained by a state of euphoria and excitement felt due to the embodiment of Shah Rukh Khan styles and works by the general population of India and fans worldwide.

One might wonder why or how this phenomenon may have been created. And this is when you want to look at the personal life of Shah who has been exceptionally caring about others, and genuine about himself and his work. He has accepted his failures as much as he has shown gratitude for his immense successes!! There is something about honesty that makes you secure and complete as a human being. And honesty is what makes Shah Rukh Khan a phenomenon. There are neither secrets nor any meretricious building of excuses on his part when his films or his attempts have not worked. And it is this magnanimity of forgiving himself or others when it has been tough is what makes Shah Rukh Khan one of the most inspiring human beings ever.

He is a good source of inspiration, and he made the right use of his power and position to lead and correct people by modelling their behaviors. Shah Rukh Khan has stood up against wrongs, whether through his films or in real life, and has never made them about himself. He has approached problems and stood by real social issues and the actor has done this with so much humility and care that people have not forgotten. The actor has never walked away from social issues or economic problems affecting the country, whether it is during the testing times of a cyclone or during the COVID-19 crisis. The actor has been doing social works and human welfare acts for ages, and real people in India who have known SRK for decades knows the generosities of the actor. The person he is, the spirit he has—the man he is on-screen and the soul he is off-screen—there is always something left to respect and love about SRK! That is why UNESCO may have found it crucial to honour his humanitarian works with Pyramide con Marni Award because the example will be set for billions of people to initiate acts of kindness and altruism that will make actual difference to the world.

If social change comprises economic, cultural, institutional, and human transformation while breaking the shackles of past mistakes and wrongs, then in the modern context, Shah Rukh Khan has been one of the torch bearers of this change in India.

From inspiring people across world to follow their dreams in life, to making larger-than-life movies, to standing up for real-life issues like poverty, women empowerment, equality, acid attack victims, treatment of cancer patients, and many others, Shah Rukh Khan is a burning example of how every person, with whatever gifts, powers, and intellect they have, can make a difference to society and world around them. 'SRK and India' remains a forever love affair, a celebration of life and happiness that gives the country its identity. You cannot separate the two, like you cannot separate day and night, rain and water, sun and light. Whenever the actor's name is taken, people will talk about their love for Shah Rukh Khan, and whenever India's name is taken, there will always be the name of Shah Rukh Khan.

For the world, SRK remains the epitome of love, and his phenomenal stardom proves that people of world across boundaries of races, languages, cultures, and continents can connect over love, goodness, and kindness. Shah Rukh Khan is a prime example of how a person should be living his life: with honesty and hard work, and if there is a god above your head, the crown will be yours at the end.

-——THE END———

About the Author

Sayan Roy is an author from India, his debut book 'Shahrukh Khan and Winds of Fire' ranked #1 in Non-fiction 'Religion and Spirituality' category of Rakuten Kobo, becoming a Bestseller worlwide. The non-fiction work based on his life memories of Shah Rukh Khan recieved critical acclaims and positive reviews from around the world. His other stories and short stories are also published in local and international magazines.

www.ingramcontent.com/pod-product-compliance
Lightning Source LLC
Chambersburg PA
CBHW051825130726
47987CB00003B/1410